MAD, Bad
and Just Plain
Dangerous
TUDORS

illustrated by
Matt Lilly

EDGE

W
FRANKLIN WATTS

First published in 2013 by Franklin Watts

Created and developed by Taglines Creative Limited
Text by John Townsend
Illustrations and layout by Matt Lilly
Cover design by Cathryn Gilbert

Franklin Watts
338 Euston Road London NW1 3BH

Franklin Watts Australia
Level 17/207 Kent Street, Sydney, NSW 2000

A CIP catalogue record for this book
is available from the British Library.

ISBN: 978 1 4451 2192 5

1 3 5 7 9 10 8 6 4 2

Printed in Great Britain

Franklin Watts is
a division of Hachette Children's Books,
an Hachette UK company.

www.hachette.co.uk

CONTENTS

Read on
or else!

Chapter 1
Terrifying Tudor Times

Welcome to the world of the Tudors. It may not be what you expect... 500 years ago could be wickedly weird, wild and wacky. Scary events made this a mad, bad and dangerous time. The 118 years that the Tudor dynasty ruled (from 1485 to 1603) were often risky and deadly. This wasn't the safest time to be alive... or even dead!

Hello, I'm Henry VIII. Come on in for a mad ride through Tudor times – be careful to hang on to your head, er... I mean hat!

King Henry the Eighth could
be scary.

And so could his daughter,
Queen Mary.

They'd find any excuse

For the axe, fire or noose

And were never just nice
or played fairly!

Tudors the Soap

So who were the Tudors?

The Tudor dynasty ruled England and Wales while another royal family, the Stuarts, ruled Scotland. In the Tudor family there were three kings followed by nearly three queens. Why 'nearly'? Tune into *Tudors – the Soap* to find out.

Cast list:

Henry VII	1485–1509
Henry VIII	1509–1547 (plus wives)
Edward VI	1547–1553
(Lady Jane Grey	'Queen' for 9 days, 10–19 July 1553)
Mary I	1553–1558
Elizabeth I	1558–1603

The midwife

The axeman

A Pope and lots of bishops

I am Lady Jane Grey and I demand a bigger part!

Watch out for...

- Henry VII planning to marry off his young son to an older woman...

- Henry VIII taking over as king – he always wants his own way. This causes serious rows with the Pope and priests in the Catholic Church...

- Henry VIII marrying six wives (not all at once)...

- BIG rows, mega fights and the mad axeman!

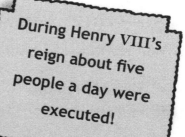

During Henry VIII's reign about five people a day were executed!

No wonder I'm always feeling so tired.

Episode 1 begins on page 12...

9

Life for ordinary people

 Girls could get married at the age of 12 and boys at 14.

About one in three children died before they were 10 years old.

 Disease and dodgy food didn't make for healthy living — nine out of 10 people died before they were 40 years old.

The drinking water was so disgusting that most people drank weak beer — even the children! The rich drank wine and sherry.

The beer I drank at breakfast had much body in it.

Tis so, sir. A dead rat did float upon it!

Stinky and itchy

The Tudors were itchy and smelly a lot of the
time. They didn't wash much or take baths.
The poor often slept on straw mattresses on mud
floors, with fleas, rats, smoke and poo all around.

Hard times

Most people in Tudor times were very poor. But
anyone who went begging, stealing birds' eggs or
poaching at night was likely to be thrown in
prison, flogged or hanged.

Tudors ☞ the Soap

Episode 1: A Father's Wish

Scene 1: A room in Richmond Palace, near London, England. Date: 1503.

Action

Henry VII: Come here, son. I need a word.

Henry Junior: What is it, Father?

Henry VII:  Since your brother Arthur died last year, I think it's a good idea if you marry his widow, Catherine. She's from Aragon in Spain so you'd help our Spanish links when you become king.

Henry Junior: But Father, I'm only 11.

Henry VII: You'll grow. She's only 18 herself!

Hope I grow quickly!

Scene 2: Henry VII's bed chamber. Date: 1509.

Action

King Henry VII aged 52:	I'm very sick and I'm about to die.
Henry Junior:	Can I help, Father?
Henry VII:	Yes! You're 18 now so make sure you marry Catherine… ergh …ugh… glglglg….. (*dies*).

Two months later the new king (Henry VIII) married Catherine of Aragon. They had a baby daughter (Mary), but Henry really wanted a son.

It's a girl!

What use is a girl? I need a son!

Why is Henry so keen to have a son? Find out in the next thrilling episode on page 16…

Chapter 2

MAD Marriages

For the first 50 years of Tudor rule, the Catholic Church was all powerful. It had lots of money, land and property. The Pope in Rome ruled the Church across Europe — including England. But Henry VIII wasn't happy about the Pope's power, especially his rules on marriage and divorce, so he made some cunning plans. Find out what happens when Henry takes on the Catholic Church and the Pope in Episode 2 of *Tudors — the Soap* coming next...

Oooh, I can't wait!

All Tudors were well used
to danger.

As Henry the Eighth
became stranger.

Especially his wife,

Who would fear for her life

As he could sharpen his axe
and exchange her!

Tudors  the Soap

Episode 2: The Takeover

Scene 1: Henry VIII was married to Catherine of Aragon for 24 years, but she did not give birth to a son that lived. Date: 1527.

Action

Henry VIII: I need a boy to be my heir.

Catherine: Unlikely, my dear.

Henry VIII: Then I want a divorce.

Catherine: The Catholic Church will not allow it.

Henry VIII: I'll ask the Pope.

I'm the Pope, and I say NO divorce!

That's what he thinks!

Scene 2: Because the Pope would not grant him a divorce, Henry planned a big religious shake-up called the Reformation. He made himself Supreme Head of the Church in England in 1534. In 1536 he began the Dissolution of the Monasteries and over the next few years closed hundreds of monasteries around the country.

Henry VIII: Ha ha!...I'll close the monasteries and grab their land and treasures.

Meanwhile, back to Henry and Catherine...

Tudors the Soap

Episode 3: Grisly Gossip

Scene 1: King Henry VIII divorced Catherine of Aragon and quickly married Anne Boleyn.

Midwife:	It's a girl!
Anne:	Let's call her Elizabeth.
Henry VIII:	Grrrr, not another girl.
	(Three years later):
Henry VIII:	Still no son. Right, I'll get rid of Anne. I'll tell everyone she's had lots of boyfriends and been too friendly with my musician, Mark Smeaton.

Yeow!
Anything you say!

Smeaton (on the rack):	Stop! All right, I admit it, I love Anne.
Axeman:	Farewell, Smeaton...*chop!*

Anne Boleyn was sent to the Tower of London. In 1536, in front of 2,000 people, her head was sliced off by a French swordsman … **chop!** Job done. King Henry was a single man once again.

The end should be quick, I only have a little neck.

WELCOME TO THE TOWER OF LONDON

According to the gossip of the day, when her head fell in the straw, Queen Anne's lips were still moving.

Who would be Henry's third wife, and more to the point, would she have a baby boy? Find out in the next episode…

Tudors the Soap

Episode 4: Worried Wives

Scene 1: Hampton Court Palace. King Henry VIII's new wife was Jane Seymour. Date: 1537.

Midwife:	It's a baby boy!
Jane:	We'll call him Edward.
Henry VIII:	I'm over the moon!
	(12 days later, Jane died):
Henry VIII:	Who shall I marry now?

I was Henry's favourite wife so we were buried together.

I could tell you so much ... but I can only speak German.

Jane Seymour

Anne of Cleves

Scene 2: Wife number four was Anne of Cleves.

Date: 1540 (6 months and 3 days after their marriage).

(Action)

Henry VIII:	Anne, you look like a horse. I only married you because you looked nice in a portrait.
Anne:	Entschuldigung! (*Pardon!*)
Henry VIII:	I fancy your maid of honour, Katherine Howard. I'm going to divorce you and marry her.

But within two years, Henry accused Katherine Howard (wife five) of loving another man and had her beheaded. Two years later he married Catherine Parr. Henry died four years later in 1547.

I lost my head!

I was more of a nurse than a wife.

Katherine Howard

Catherine Parr

But the Tudor story is not over yet. Look out for the next mad episode on page 30!

Was Henry VIII mad?

When Henry was 35, he had a bad jousting accident. The wounds to both legs developed smelly, painful ulcers. The ulcers had to be cut (more pain) and rubbed with cream. Lead in the cream poisoned his blood and could have made him go mad.

Henry aged 57

Henry got worse over the years.

If his doctors had told him that he was dying or going mad they were certain to lose their heads.

Bigger and madder

Henry VIII had all sorts of illnesses as he got older. Towards the end of his life Henry was so overweight he had to be carried to bed! He weighed about 180 kg and his huge waist measured a mega 132 cm.

Come along, Your Highness, time for beddy-byes.

It's likely that Henry's terrible pain and treatments made him go a bit bonkers.

Team up with friends or try the quiz yourself to see if you would survive in Tudor times. Add up your scores for each answer. When you've done all the quizzes, check out the final results on page 88.

1. Do you like having a bath?

A Every day

B Sometimes

C Never

---

2. Do you like rats?

A They're cute

B Not bothered

C Eek!

---

3. Would you bow to the king?

A Definitely

B Certainly not

C Maybe

Scores for answers:

1. A = 0   B = 5   C = 9 (You'd be a happy Tudor if you didn't like baths)
2. A = 4   B = 9   C = 1 (You'd be a happier Tudor if you didn't mind rats)
3. A = 8   B = 0   C = 2 (You'd be a safer Tudor if you pleased the royals)

Chapter 3

BAD Beliefs

We witches get blamed for everything...

In Tudor times, disease and death were everywhere. When people couldn't explain bad things they used magic, superstitions or religion to help them. When things went very wrong, they blamed witches, spirits, God, the Church or even the royals.

Despite all their fine
Tudor riches,

The royals had hiccups
and hitches...

So when things went wrong,

It didn't take long

To go out and burn a
few witches.

Wicked witches

People believed witches cast spells that made bad things happen. In 1542, new laws made witchcraft a crime. Anyone thought to be making spells could be put to death, even people using herbs for homemade cures. Someone with a warty nose, an unusual birthmark, a black cat or even a broomstick could be accused of being a witch!

They think I'm a witch so I'm hiding in here until they've gone.

Wet witches

A person accused of being a witch could be tied to a ducking stool — a see-saw with a chair that was swung over a pond. The accused was tied to the chair and dunked under the water until she confessed to being a witch.

A worse punishment for witches was being tied in a sack and thrown in a river. If the victim floated, she was guilty and would be burned to death. If she sank, she was innocent ... but dead!

Tudors  the Soap

Episode 5: Killer Queens

Scene 1: While witch hunters searched the land for little old ladies, Henry's son was crowned King Edward VI when he was just nine years old. Date: 1547.

Action

Bishop: You don't look well, Your Highness.

Edward VI: I'll be fine if I please God. I'll start by making churches much simpler. Get rid of all the decorations, paintings and stained glass.

Bishop: If you insist, your majesty.

(Six years later):

Edward VI in bed Ergh…. ugh… glglglg….. *(dies)*

Gossip: I reckon the King upset God. Or maybe a witch cast a spell.

> Actually I died of TB.

Scene 2: Most people expected Edward's half sister, Mary, to be next on the throne. Date: 1553.

Action

John Dudley (chief councillor to the King): We can't have Mary as queen, she's a Catholic. Edward wanted his cousin, Lady Jane Grey, to follow him so quick, make her queen. She's a Protestant so she can marry my son.

Jane: So now I'm married and queen, and I'm only 16!

(Nine days later):

Mary I: What's going on? I'm Henry VIII's daughter so I should be queen. The people want me, not Jane. Off with her head!

Axeman: John Dudley *Chop!*
Jane's hubby *Chop!*
Lady Jane *Chop!*

I never even got to wear the crown!

Tudors  the Soap

Episode 6: Cruel Cousin

Scene 1: Mary I set about getting rid of the new Protestant religion and making England Roman Catholic again. Date: 1553.

Mary I:	Does anyone disagree with my Catholic views?
Bishops:	Yes, the Protestants!
Mary I:	Fair enough. You'll all be burnt to death.
Bishops:	No wonder they call her Bloody Mary. Aaaah! *(sizzle, cough, woosh)*

Mary had over 280 Protestants burned at the stake. But, in 1558, after just over four years as queen, Mary I died, aged 42.

> **My favourite hobby is executing bishops. Such fun!**

Now it was the turn of the last Tudor royal…

Scene 2: In 1558, Elizabeth I was crowned queen. Her 45-year reign was called 'The Golden Age', but there were still problems about religion. One big problem was Elizabeth's cousin, Mary Queen of Scots. Date: 1568.

Action

Mary (writing):	Dear Cousin Elizabeth, I must flee from Scotland as I fear there is a plot against me.
Elizabeth I (reading the letter):	A plot against Mary? That's because she's Catholic. Ha ha..
Bishop:	But if Mary comes to England, a lot of people would want a Catholic queen like her.
Elizabeth I:	Really? In that case – lock her up!

All this stress is making me feel ruff!

Scene 3: Mary is still in prison. Date: 1587.

Action

Elizabeth I: I've been told it's about time I signed Mary's death warrant.

Axeman: Here goes, Mary… ***Thwack!*** Oops, not quite. ***Thwack!*** Oops, still not quite. ***Chop!*** That's better. I'll lift up the head… oops, the wig's come off… oops, the head's bouncing!

Oops, Mary lost her head … now I've lost it!

What's next for Elizabeth I? Look out for Episode 7, on page 44…

Team up with friends or try the quiz yourself to see if you would survive in Tudor times. Add up your scores for each answer. When you've done all the quizzes, check out the final results on page 88.

1. Do you believe in good and bad luck?

A Yes, touch wood!

B Sometimes

C Never

2. Do you like cats?

A They're great pets

B I adore them

C Keep them away from me

3. Do you go wobbly at the sight of blood?

A Sometimes

B Yuck, I'm squeamish

C I love gory stuff

Scores for answers:

1. A = 0 B = 5 C = 9 (It could be risky being a superstitious Tudor)

2. A = 3 B = 1 C = 9 (Cat lovers could be accused of being a witch)

3. A = 4 B = 1 C = 9 (For some jobs, eg axeman, you'd need a strong stomach)

Chapter 4

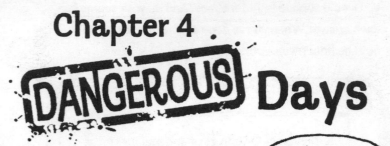

DANGEROUS Days

Life was dangerous for everyone in Tudor times. Whatever you were doing – playing sport, at work or travelling – you could be sure health and safety rules didn't matter.

I'm not leaving the house – it's much too dangerous!

When Elizabeth

came to the throne,

Health and safety at work

was unknown.

The axeman got busy,

For the fussy Queen Lizzy

Oops! He was terribly

accident-prone.

Mad matches

Football was very popular with the ordinary people, who sometimes went a bit wild and attacked each other during the game. Players were often hurt or even killed in violent matches. A Tudor writer reported: *"Football is more a fight than a game ... sometimes their necks are broken, sometimes their backs, sometimes their legs ... football encourages envy and hatred ... sometimes fighting, murder and a great loss of blood."*

The football was a blown up pig's bladder!

No way....

> I've played for five hours, run for miles and the score is still 0–0.

> In a tackle, two Tudor footballers accidentally stabbed themselves with a knife.

Time's up!

Tudor football wasn't quite like it is today. The pitch could stretch from one village to another so each team's goals could be miles apart. Players could pick up the ball and run with it, and they wore no protective gear. Teams had far more than 11 players, and games lasted for hours.

Perilous pastime

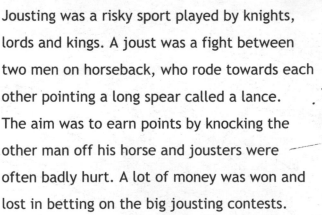

Oi, mind my helmet!

Jousting was a risky sport played by knights, lords and kings. A joust was a fight between two men on horseback, who rode towards each other pointing a long spear called a lance. The aim was to earn points by knocking the other man off his horse and jousters were often badly hurt. A lot of money was won and lost in betting on the big jousting contests.

Dangerous jousting

In 1520, King Henry VIII and King Francis I of France wanted to make peace between their countries, so they had a joust. One of Henry's men broke Francis's nose. Oops!

In 1536, Henry VIII fell from his horse during a joust, then the horse fell on him. The king was in full heavy armour and so was his horse. Henry was knocked unconscious for two hours. The court thought he would die but he pulled through — but he was never quite the same again.

Fatal farm work

Records from the 1550s tell of horrific farm accidents, such as workers crushed, sliced and squashed by watermills, windmills and heavy carts.

 A boy fell asleep by a haystack, which collapsed and suffocated him.

 A five-year-old pig herder in Yorkshire was killed by his animals.

 A butcher's boy was bringing a horse-load of meat through London when he fell into a pit by the road and was killed.

Watch out!

Tree-climbing was common among peasants because they needed to collect fruit, nuts and birds' eggs to eat, or acorns to feed their pigs. Records show that many were killed and injured falling out of trees.

Horse horrors

Horses caused 90 per cent of animal accidents. People were killed falling off, being dragged along, trampled or kicked to death. Ouch!

Tudors the Soap

Episode 7: Quarrelsome Queen

Scene 1: Everyday life might have been mad, but the reign of Elizabeth I was a time of great progress. Exploration, trade and the arts developed like never before. But there was a catch... Elizabeth made England Protestant again, which caused trouble with King Philip of Spain (dead Queen Mary I's husband) who decided to invade and take the English throne for Spain. Date: 1588.

King Philip II of Spain: I'm sending 130 of my warships to attack England with 2,500 guns and 30,000 men. Ha ha, my navy is bigger than yours – and you're just a woman.

Elizabeth I: I've got the heart and stomach of a king – so watch it!

Superior English ships and fighting skills and bad weather defeated the Spanish Armada.

RESULT: England 1, Spain 0

Scene 2: Queen Elizabeth had many enemies. As she got older she thought assassins were waiting round every corner to kill her. Date: 1603.

Action

Elizabeth I: I've never had a husband to look after me. That's why I carry a sword. And watch out, I've got a fiery temper. Even though I'm not well, I'm not going to my bed. Keep the doctors away!

Ugh, perhaps I iwll lie down for a little while, ergh…. ugh… glglglg….. *(dies)*.

The Tudor age is over!

The end!

Mary Queen of Scots' son, James, King of Scotland, becomes King of England and the Stuart dynasty begins – but that's another story.

Team up with friends or try the quiz yourself to see if you would survive in Tudor times. Add up your scores for each answer. When you've done all the quizzes, check out the final results on page 88.

1. Do you like playing football?

A Yes – lots

B Sometimes

C Never

2. Would you like to try jousting?

A Not likely

B Definitely

C Maybe worth a try

3. Do you spend much time in the countryside?

A Yes

B No

C I've been on a farm

Scores for answers:

1. A = 1   B = 5   C = 10 (It could be very risky playing Tudor football!)
2. A = 10   B = 1   C = 7 (Tudor jousting could be very high risk!)
3. A = 1   B = 9   C = 2 (Living in the countryside was very risky)

Chapter 5

MAD Medicine

The Tudors had all sorts of mad, bad and dangerous treatments for illness. Just as well because they had some pretty gross diseases, such as the bubonic plague, which killed thousands of people. Be warned … the following medical madness might make you need a lie-down!

When the Tudors caught just
a slight chill,

They'd most likely become
very ill

With something quite chronic

Or grossly bubonic

With black bloated boils
that could kill (yuck)!

Barbaric barbers

Guess where most sick people went to get treatment? To the hairdresser's! Barber surgeons were sort of superior barbers who could perform operations. Basic barbers could only bleed patients (see page 54 for the revolting details) and pull out teeth.

This won't hurt – well, not much!

Ouch!

Tudor barber surgeons didn't have anaesthetic to give to patients, so strong helpers had to hold patients down. When sawing off a rotting limb, the surgeon would often make the patient drunk first to help dull the pain.

Boil bother

Barbers used red-hot irons to burn out infected wounds. If anyone had a nasty boil, the barber would heat up a needle and prod the boil till it burst. Yeow!

Hmm, I'll try the red-hot irons.

To find out what was wrong with patients, a barber would swirl their urine in a jar. The colour, smell and, yes ... TASTE would tell him what treatment to give.

Things you did not want to hear at the barbers...

"Pass the vinegar." Vinegar was rubbed on wounds because it helped to kill disease. It would sting like mad and make the patient smell like a pickled onion!

You'll soon get the point of this treatment...

"Right, bend over!" A special syringe was used during the early Tudor period to pump liquid up a patient's bottom. It helped to clear blockages! Liquid medicine, or warm water, was squirted into the patient's body using a plunger inserted into the top of a tube.

This will help... NOT!

Barber surgeons worked on Henry VIII's ship, the
Mary Rose. Sometimes they injected diseased
patients with a poisonous metal called mercury.
This treatment was very dangerous because
mercury makes you go mad. A syringe for giving this
treatment was found on the wreck of the *Mary Rose*.

Bad blood

The Tudors thought that some people got sick because they had 'bad' blood. So all you had to do if you felt poorly was drop in on the barber and he would do a bit of 'bloodletting'. This meant cutting a vein so the blood squirted out and the 'bad' came out with the blood.

Leeches — GROSS!

leech

If you didn't like the idea of having your skin cut, there was another way to be bled. The barber would slap a few leeches over your body and the slimy creatures would drink your blood instead. Well, the leeches enjoyed it!

Blood...
yum, yum!

Warning!
Bloodletting was not good first aid and was very dodgy medicine. In fact, bloodletting probably killed more people than it 'cured'. If you see this on offer in a barber's shop today, give Health and Safety a call and run!

Plague and pox

Everyone was afraid of bubonic plague, or the Black Death. It caused fever and big black swellings on the armpits and legs. Most victims died within a few days. It was treated by cutting the swellings with a needle, then slapping on a hot mixture of butter, onion and garlic. This did no good at all, but it smelt delicious.

Does my nose look big in this?

Doctors wore long gowns and a mask with a beak that had strong-smelling herbs inside. They thought this would stop them from catching the smelly disease. It didn't!

Scarred for life

Smallpox was a deadly disease during Tudor times. Victims often died covered with festering blisters. Those who survived could be blinded or have terrible scars left all over their face and body.

Doctor, will my spots get better?

I never make RASH promises.

Queen Elizabeth I caught smallpox in 1562. She was lucky to survive. She always wore thick white make up (made from lead!) to hide the scars and pockmarks on her face.

Creepy cures

The Tudors had all sorts of creepy and crazy cures:

For gout — make a mixture of boiled-up worms, pigs marrow, herbs and a red-haired dog. Rub onto the foot.

Breathing difficulties — swallow frogs greased with butter so they slip down easily.

For baldness — shave the head and smear the grease from a fox onto the scalp. Crush a garlic bulb and rub it into the scalp, followed by vinegar.

Can you give me something for wind?

How about a kite?

Team up with friends or try the quiz yourself to see if you would survive in Tudor times. Add up your scores for each answer. When you've done all the quizzes, check out the final results on page 88.

1. Are you scared of going to the dentist?

A Never

B Sometimes

C Big time!

2. Could you touch a live leech?

A Easy – no problem

B No thanks

C AAGH don't go there!

3. Do you go wobbly at the sight of YOUR blood?

A Sometimes

B No problem

C Eek – I daren't even think about it

Scores for answers:

1. A = 10 B = 5 C = 1 (Tudor dentists (barbers) were much scarier than today)
2. A = 10 B = 3 C = 0 (You might have to have leeches put on your body)
3. A = 4 B = 9 C = 1 (For some treatments you'd have to be 'bled'.)

Chapter 6

BAD Behaviour

Breaking Tudor laws was a dangerous business. Punishments were grim and carried out in public. Executions were common. Everyone shuddered at the thought of being sent to the Tower of London — it was filled with evil instruments of torture that were used to make people confess to things they hadn't even done!

STOP! STOP! I did it, whatever it was.

As a Tudor accused of
a crime,

You would dread being killed
in your prime.

Being hanged, drawn and
quartered

And publicly slaughtered

Was such a bad waste of
your time!

Gruesome warnings

Anyone caught stealing anything worth more than a few pennies risked a death sentence. Even a starving boy taking a few birds' eggs from a nest on a noble's land could be hanged.

Gossips, usually women, were forced to wear a terrible mask called a scold's bridle. Nosy people were made to wear a mask with a long nose and sharp spikes inside the mouthpiece.

Grmp mhgrar glur garph!

Grisly day out

To remind people that crime didn't pay, Tudors held public executions. You could watch a few hangings, witches being burnt alive or hear poisoners scream as they were boiled alive in huge pots of water. Then, on the way home, you could count the rotting heads of traitors stuck on poles along London Bridge.

This wind is really messing up my hair.

Beggars and burglars

Anyone roaming the country without a job could be tied to a cart and whipped "till they be bloody". If that didn't stop them, beggars or vagabonds could have a hole burned through an ear or end up in prison. That's if they were lucky. If not, they were sent to be hanged.

The problem was that many jobless people had no choice but to wander around trying to find work.

I'm so poor I'm having a whip round...

I used to hang around crowds and cut purses. Then they caught me and now I'm just hanging around!

Stop thief!

As Tudors had no pockets they carried money in cloth or leather pouches round their waists. Thieves, known as cutpurses, could easily cut the pouch or strings and run off with the money.

Another common crime was 'hooking'. Not many windows had glass so burglars with hooks on long poles would reach inside rooms to hook out purses and run off ... to the gallows if they were caught!

Pain and punishment

If thieves weren't hanged, they might have the letter 'T' burned into their flesh with a red-hot iron. But that's not all. Some criminals had their ears cut off, nostrils slit and hands chopped off.

He's had more that his five-a-day of rotten fruit!

Tudors clamped rowdy troublemakers in a pillory in the middle of town. Then everyone would hurl insults or rotten food at them!

Look away now!

Being hanged, drawn and quartered was a nasty punishment for treason. After being dragged through the streets by a horse, the prisoner was hanged. Just before choking to death, he was sliced open and his intestines pulled out and cooked in front of him. The body was cut into quarters and the pieces displayed as a warning to others.

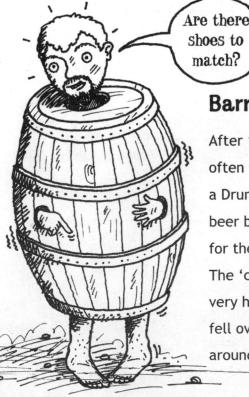

Are there shoes to match?

Barrel of laughs

After 1551, drunks were often forced to wear a Drunkard's Cloak — a beer barrel with holes for the arms and legs. The 'cloak' could get very heavy and if they fell over they just rolled around.

Terror in the Tower

The Tower of London was where traitors were imprisoned and tortured. Prisoners were dragged to the horrifying torture chambers through the dreaded Traitor's Gate.

In 1546, Anne Askew didn't agree with Henry VIII's religious beliefs and said so. Mistake! She was sent to the Tower to be tortured, but she refused to name the others who shared her beliefs. She was carried off the rack and burnt at the stake, still saying, "I would rather die than break my faith."

NO!
Don't take me through that gate.

TRAITOR'S GATE

You will talk!

John Gerard was a priest and a spy who was accused of trying to get rid of Queen Elizabeth I. He was sent to the Tower.

Ergh, that's digusting!

I feel sick!

We cannot show this picture because it is too gruesome.

"They ... left me hanging by my hands and arms fastened above my head. All the blood in my body seemed to rush up into my arms and hands and I thought that blood was oozing from the ends of my fingers."

Despite the pain, Gerard refused to talk and managed to escape.

Team up with friends or try the quiz yourself to see if you would survive in Tudor times. Add up your scores for each answer. When you've done all the quizzes, check out the final results on page 88.

1. Are you always good?

A I'm an angel

B Usually OK

C I get told off lots

2. Do you like a bit of juicy gossip?

A Not really

B Now and again

C Ooh, you bet!

3. Do you squeal if you get hurt?

A No – I'm always calm

B Yes – I don't do pain

C I might cry

Scores for answers:

1. A = 9 B = 5 C = 1 (It could be dead risky getting into trouble)

2. A = 9 B = 6 C = 2 (Gossips could be punished in Tudor times)

3. A = 8 B = 1 C = 6 (You'd need nerves of steel if you were tortured)

Chapter 7

DANGEROUS

Dirt and Disease

Tudor towns were grubby, smelly, smoky and risky. Streets were full of animal dung, human waste, rats, fleas, flies and lice. Without proper drains, sewers or toilets, Tudors had to watch where they were treading! Tudor homes had earth floors and people ate from wooden plates and bowls that were difficult to keep clean without hot running water and washing-up liquid. Life was dirty and dangerous.

Mmm, nice!

If you ever turn into
a Tudor,

Your trips to the loo will
be cruder.

As you'd go in the street,

Over somebody's feet,

You'd be madder and badder
and ruder!

Wicked waste

'Gong' was the word for a toilet and its contents. A toilet was usually a pot in the corner or a hole in the ground outside. Poor people would use leaves or moss to wipe their Tudor bottoms.

The pit full of stinking waste would get emptied at night by gong farmers. Some Tudor children worked for the gong farmers. They had to spread buckets of 'night soil' over crops. If they fainted from the smell they would fall in the cesspit.

Phew!
I should be
called a PONG
farmer!

Smelly end

A report tells of a baker from Cambridge who met a grisly and pongy end. On 2nd June 1523, after drinking too much beer, he went to have a wee in a cesspit. Oh no, ... he staggered, slipped and fell headfirst into the seething night soil. And that was where the gong farmer found his smelly remains the next day. YUCK!

Festering filth

Without proper toilets, some Tudor peasants would wee in the street. Others would empty their chamber pots out of their windows with a cry of "Gardez l'eau!" That's French for "watch out for the water". Our word 'loo' may have come from this Tudor warning.

Gardez l'eau!

It looks like rain.

It doesn't smell like it!

Top bottoms

Rich people used lamb's wool to wipe their bottoms. Royalty had servants to wipe their bottoms for them. A royal bottom-wiper was called 'the Groom of the Stool'.

My career has started at the very bottom!

King Henry VIII's privy had a padded seat made with silk ribbons and gold studs. His servants at Hampton Court weren't so lucky. They all had to go together on a 28-seater. Friendly!

Grubby, grotty and gross

Wearing thick Tudor clothes could be very sweaty. Smelling fresh wasn't easy without deodorant or detergent. Clothes might have to last a long time before being washed. In other words, most people stank! The only Tudors to have proper bathrooms were the very rich, but even Queen Elizabeth only took a bath about once every three months.

Deadly bites

flea · · · · · △

Typhus was a nasty fever and rash that was common in dirty, overcrowded places, such as Tudor homes. It was spread by fleas or lice biting a person to suck their blood. The insect left a dropping, the person scratched the bite and the dropping went into the wound causing infection. Gross!

I've just had my annual bath.

Happy bathday!

People in Tudor times could die from typhus, but those who took baths and boiled their clothes were far more likely to keep typhus away.

Terrifying teeth

Most Tudors had dodgy teeth. There were no proper toothbrushes or toothpaste, and rich people liked a lot of sugar. This rotted their teeth and turned them black. Some people even blackened their teeth with soot to make themselves look rich!

One tooth-cleaner was made of mouse heads. The heads were cooked in a pan until they burned, and then ground into a gritty powder. The powder was sprinkled on a rag and rubbed on the teeth.

Not very minty — just mousy!

Pooh! What you need is a good 'mouse' wash!

Team up with friends or try the quiz yourself to see if you would survive in Tudor times. Add up your scores for each answer. When you've done all the quizzes, check out the final results on page 88.

1. Can you cope with revolting smells?

A No — nothing gross for me

B No big deal

C I love 'em!

2. Are you fussy about your personal hygiene?

A Not too bothered

B I'm always sweet-smelling

C I have to be spotless

3. Have you got a sweet tooth?

A Yum to fizzy drinks

B I only eat healthy food

C I adore sweets

Scores for answers:

1. A = 0 B = 5 C = 9 (You'd have to cope with nasty smells as a Tudor!)

2. A = 9 B = 5 C = 0 (Tudors couldn't be fussy)

3. A = 2 B = 9 C = 1 (Tudors who liked sugar got bad, black teeth)

Chapter 8
Final Fears

Death was a big topic for the Tudors. It was all around them and they knew it could strike at any moment. One of the big fears for the dying was if they would go to hell and burn, or spend eternity as tormented ghosts! Many of the plays performed in Tudor theatres were about tragedy, murder and ghosts. Shakespeare wrote about these in some of his plays.

I went to a play about death and laughed my head off!

Queen Elizabeth gasped her
last breath,

And people were stunned by
her death.

It was left to Shakespeare

To bring laughter and cheer

So he wrote that rib-tickler
'Macbeth!'*

*(In fact, it's dead scary, full of blood, murder and ghosts.)

Unhappy endings

Within days of dying, people were buried in a churchyard. This was 'hallowed ground' or a holy place where souls would be safe. But graveyards were not always big enough when too many people died at the same time, so bones and skulls were dug up to make room for new bodies. Many churchyards became so full that old bones were stored in a charnel house, a special place for bones, behind a church.

I didn't think we'd have to share.

Living dead

People who killed themselves couldn't be buried in a churchyard. Instead they were buried in land not blessed by the church. It was believed that suicides and sailors buried at sea were more likely to become ghosts, because their burial ground was unholy.

Rich people were sometimes buried inside a church under the floor to show how important they were... and it was much warmer there!

This graveyard's freezing. I'm off to find somewhere warmer.

Fatal finish

You might still meet a few famous Tudors today. Stories tell of shrieks, groans, cries and the rattle of chains coming from the dungeons in the Tower of London! Some nights, people say they have seen the ghosts of famous women who were beheaded at the Tower, such as Anne Boleyn, Katherine Howard and Lady Jane Grey.

Wooooo! Aaargh!

Is that the rattle of chains I can hear?

No, it's the rattle of my knees.

Haunted Hampton Court

It's not just the Tower of London that has ghosts. In Hampton Court Palace, Katherine Howard is said to walk the Haunted Gallery where she was dragged screaming and pleading for her life.

One evening, two visitors fainted on exactly the same spot in the Haunted Gallery, just half an hour apart. A member of staff said, "Things do happen in the Haunted Gallery. I was being interviewed for a radio programme when the recording machine suddenly switched itself off ...". Spooky!

What is your total score from the Survival Quizzes at the end of the chapters? Add up your points from all 18 questions to see how long you would survive under the Tudors.

Over 150	WOW — you'd make a great Tudor! Your chances of making it to old age are promising. There again, were your answers strictly honest?
100 — 150	Fairly good. You're a Tudor with a fair chance of reaching your 40th birthday. Just.
80 — 100	Not bad. You'd make a fairly average Tudor but don't plan for old age.
50 — 80	Ooer — you're high risk. Tudor life isn't for you. Low survival chances.
Below 50	AAH! Give up now. You wouldn't make a successful Tudor. Only a dead one.

If your scores were a whole mixture, that means you'd probably be a fairly normal Tudor. You'd have no idea if or when something horrible would strike ... such as an axe ... in fact, the axeman is already on his way...

So what dost thou make of all this Tudor stuff?

Verily, it all be mad, bad and just plain mega dangerous!

Dramatic Dates

1485   Henry VII is crowned – the first Tudor king.

1499   Plague kills thousands of people in London.

1509   Henry VII dies (not from plague but there's still a lot about). His son, Henry VIII, is crowned king. Henry VIII marries his dead brother's wife, Catherine of Aragon. The marriage lasts 24 years but there is no male heir.

1533   The Pope refuses to grant Henry a divorce from Catherine so Henry annuls, or cancels, the marriage himself and marries Anne Boleyn (she gives birth to Elizabeth the same year).

1536-40 Henry VIII closes Catholic monasteries and takes their treasures and sells their land. He makes himself head of the Church of England.

1537   Anne Boleyn beheaded. Henry VIII marries Jane Seymour 11 days after Anne's execution. Later the same year Jane has a son (Edward VI). Jane dies less than two weeks later.

1540   Henry VIII marries Anne of Cleves as part of a Protestant alliance or agreement (divorces six months later). Days after his divorce, Henry marries Katherine Howard, a cousin of Anne Boleyn. Henry is 49 years old and Katherine is 19 (she is beheaded in 1542).

1543   Henry VIII marries wife number six, Catherine Parr, who outlives him.

1545	France tries to invade England. Henry VIII's warship the *Mary Rose* sinks in Portsmouth Harbour – up to 500 sailors are killed.
1547	Henry VIII dies. His son Edward (from his third wife, Jane Seymour) becomes king aged nine.
1547–53	Edward VI reigns for six years. He dies aged 15 of TB (tuberculosis).
1553	Edward's cousin, Lady Jane Grey, becomes 'queen' for nine days. She is beheaded and replaced by Mary Tudor (Henry VIII's eldest daughter) who is crowned Mary I.
1554	Mary marries the Catholic king of Spain, Philip II.
1558	Queen Mary dies. Henry VIII's daughter by Anne Boleyn is crowned Elizabeth I.
1577	Francis Drake sails around the world (to explore, not to escape the Tudors)!
1587	England and Spain are at war. Mary Queen of Scots is charged with plotting to kill Elizabeth I and is beheaded.
1588	King Philip II organises an armada of ships to invade England but is defeated.
1590s	Shakespeare puts on his first plays in London. More plagues.
1603	Queen Elizabeth I dies and the Tudor dynasty ends. King James of Scotland becomes the first Stuart king of England as James I. He inherits a country in debt (and lots of beautiful dresses).

Gruesome Glossary

ale a type of beer

anaesthetic a chemical or gas that sends someone into deep sleep. It is used by surgeons before they perform operations.

apothecary a maker or seller of drugs and medicines

armada a large fleet of warships

assassin someone who murders an important person or leader

bladder a pouch inside the body for storing urine (liquid waste)

bubonic plague a deadly disease spread from rats to humans by fleas, causing fever, weakness and black swellings

Catholic (Roman) a branch of the Christian church led by the Pope in Rome

charnel house a building or vault where corpses or bones are piled

court (royal) the king and queen's household, including all the nobles, advisors and staff

dynasty a series of rulers of the same family or line of descent

flog to beat someone with a stick or whip

gall a bitter greenish-brown fluid stored in the body's gallbladder

gallows a structure from which criminals were hanged

gout painful swelling, especially of the feet

heir a person who carries on a title or position when the current holder dies

Ok, ok I'll learn these words!

loot(ed) to steal or take by force

marrow yellowish fatty jelly found inside some bones

midwife a nurse who helps women in childbirth

monastery a place where monks live and work

poaching hunting or fishing illegally

Protestant a member of the Christian church that separated from the Roman Catholic Church in the 16th century

rack an instrument of torture that painfully stretches the body

Reformation religious changes made in the 16th century, which led to setting up Protestant churches in England

superstition a belief people have when they fear the unknown

TB short for tuberculosis, a disease that killed thousands of people in Tudor times

traitor someone who betrays another's trust

treason the crime of trying to overthrow the government of one's country or of plotting to harm the ruler

ulcer a slow-healing sore

Weird Websites

Pssst. There's something you need to know.
This book is a fun look at just some of the mad, bad and dangerous Tudor goings-on. But there were also many great, good and glorious Tudors, too. In fact, we've got the Tudors to thank for all sorts.
Take a peep at:

www.glorioustudors.co.uk
Good and glorious Tudory stuff and some great inventions.

http://www.bbc.co.uk/history/british/tudors/
Want to know more?
Check out this site.

http://www.tudorbritain.org/
Interactive stuff to test your Tudor know-how

http://www.hrp.org.uk/
HamptonCourtPalace/
stories/palacehighlights/
ALivingTudorWorld.aspx

Infernal Index

Want to know what's in the wheelbarrow? Go to page 74.

978 1 4451 2191 8 pb   978 1 4451 2195 6 eBook

978 1 4451 2192 5 pb   978 1 4451 2196 3 eBook

978 1 4451 2193 2 pb   978 1 4451 2239 7 eBook

978 1 4451 2194 9 pb   978 1 4451 2240 3 eBook